Samoyed Dogs

Samoyed Dog Facts & Information

Samoyed Dog Cost, Buying, Rescue, Temperment, Breeding, Health, Care, Diet, Grooming, Training, And Much More!

By Lolly Brown

Foreword

The Samoyed is a medium-sized dog known for its thick white coat and friendly personality. These dogs are incredibly beautiful, both inside and out, but they are also a very intelligent and hard-working breed. If you are looking for a dog that responds well to training and loves to be around people, the Samoyed just might be the right breed for you and your family.

If you are considering the Samoyed dog for yourself or your family, do yourself a favor and learn as much as you can about these lovely dogs. The Samoyed is a wonderful breed but it is not the right choice for everyone. The more you learn about these dogs, the more equipped you will be to decide if they are the right option for you. If you decide that a Samoyed is a good fit, you will find the information you need in this book to help prepare you to become the best dog owner you can be.

If you are ready to learn more about the Samoyed breed, turn the page and keep reading!

Table of Contents

Introduction

When you look at the fluffy white Samoyed it is not difficult to imagine that he is a friendly, people-oriented breed. But can you picture him pulling a sled loaded to the brim with goods or herding reindeer through drifts of snow? While the Samoyed is certainly an excellent household pet, this breed was actually developed for some very unique purposes. These dogs are very intelligent and highly active which means that they require a certain degree of experience and a lot of attention to care for them properly.

The Samoyed is not necessarily a high-maintenance breed but it is certainly not the right breed for everyone. Not only do these dogs require a good deal of daily exercise and mental stimulation, but they have a tendency to bark a lot and they can become destructive if they get bored or lonely. The Samoyed's plush white coat also needs a lot of brushing and grooming to keep shedding under control. Before you decide whether this is the right breed for you, do yourself a favor and learn as much as you can about these dogs.

If you want to learn more about the Samoyed breed – both the good and bad – you have come to the right place. Within the pages of this book you will receive a wealth of information about the beautiful Samoyed breed as well as some key facts and the history of the breed. The more you learn about these dogs, the better equipped you will be to decide if they are the right dog for you. If you think that the Samoyed is a good fit, this book will provide you with the information you need to get started and to help you on your way to becoming the best dog owner you can be.

So, if you are ready to learn more about the Samoyed breed simply turn the page and keep reading!

Glossary of Dog Terms

AKC – American Kennel Club, the largest purebred dog registry in the United States

Almond Eye – Referring to an elongated eye shape rather than a rounded shape

Apple Head – A round-shaped skull

Balance – A show term referring to all of the parts of the dog, both moving and standing, which produce a harmonious image

Beard – Long, thick hair on the dog's underjaw

Best in Show – An award given to the only undefeated dog left standing at the end of judging

Bitch – A female dog

Bite – The position of the upper and lower teeth when the dog's jaws are closed; positions include level, undershot, scissors, or overshot

Blaze – A white stripe running down the center of the face between the eyes

Board – To house, feed, and care for a dog for a fee

Breed – A domestic race of dogs having a common gene pool and characterized appearance/function

Breed Standard – A published document describing the look, movement, and behavior of the perfect specimen of a particular breed

Buff – An off-white to gold coloring

Clip – A method of trimming the coat in some breeds

Coat – The hair covering of a dog; some breeds have two coats, and outer coat and undercoat; also known as a double coat. Examples of breeds with double coats include German Shepherd, Siberian Husky, Akita, etc.

Condition – The health of the dog as shown by its skin, coat, behavior, and general appearance

Crate – A container used to house and transport dogs; also called a cage or kennel

Crossbreed (Hybrid) – A dog having a sire and dam of two different breeds; cannot be registered with the AKC

Dam (bitch) – The female parent of a dog;

Dock – To shorten the tail of a dog by surgically removing the end part of the tail.

Double Coat – Having an outer weather-resistant coat and a soft, waterproof coat for warmth; see above.

Drop Ear – An ear in which the tip of the ear folds over and hangs down; not prick or erect

Entropion – A genetic disorder resulting in the upper or lower eyelid turning in

Fancier – A person who is especially interested in a particular breed or dog sport

Fawn – A red-yellow hue of brown

Feathering – A long fringe of hair on the ears, tail, legs, or body of a dog

Groom – To brush, trim, comb or otherwise make a dog's coat neat in appearance

Heel – To command a dog to stay close by its owner's side

Hip Dysplasia – A condition characterized by the abnormal formation of the hip joint

Inbreeding – The breeding of two closely related dogs of one breed

Kennel – A building or enclosure where dogs are kept

Litter – A group of puppies born at one time

Markings – A contrasting color or pattern on a dog's coat

Mask – Dark shading on the dog's foreface

Mate – To breed a dog and a bitch

Neuter – To castrate a male dog or spay a female dog

Pads – The tough, shock-absorbent skin on the bottom of a dog's foot

Parti-Color – A coloration of a dog's coat consisting of two or more definite, well-broken colors; one of the colors must be white

Pedigree – The written record of a dog's genealogy going back three generations or more

Pied – A coloration on a dog consisting of patches of white and another color

Prick Ear – Ear that is carried erect, usually pointed at the tip of the ear

Puppy – A dog under 12 months of age

Purebred – A dog whose sire and dam belong to the same breed and who are of unmixed descent

Saddle – Colored markings in the shape of a saddle over the back; colors may vary

Shedding – The natural process whereby old hair falls off the dog's body as it is replaced by new hair growth.

Sire – The male parent of a dog

Smooth Coat – Short hair that is close-lying

Spay – The surgery to remove a female dog's ovaries, rendering her incapable of breeding

Trim – To groom a dog's coat by plucking or clipping

Undercoat – The soft, short coat typically concealed by a longer outer coat

Wean – The process through which puppies transition from subsisting on their mother's milk to eating solid food

Whelping – The act of birthing a litter of puppies

Chapter One: Understanding Samoyeds

The first thing that many people notice about the Samoyed breed is its fluffy white coat. While the Samoyed's coat certainly is beautiful and unique, there are many more qualities to love in this breed. If you really want to determine whether this breed is a good fit for you and your family, you need to take the time to learn as much as you can about these dogs. In this chapter you will receive a general overview of the breed as well as some in-depth facts and information about Samoyeds. You will also receive a breed history to help you get started in familiarizing yourself with the Samoyed dog breed.

Facts About Samoyed Dogs

If you know anything about other Spitz-type breeds like the Alaskan Malamute and the Siberian Husky, the Samoyed may look a little familiar to you. Most Spitz-type dogs have thick double coats and a plumed tail that they carry high up over their backs. These dogs are adapted to living and working on very cold climates, relying on their wooly undercoats to keep them warm and their longer outer coats to protect them against the elements. The Samoyed is a Spitz-type dog so it has these same qualities among many others which make it unique.

There is no denying that the Samoyed, affectionately nicknamed the Sammy, is one of the most beautiful dog breeds out there. These dogs have a thick, fluffy coat that is pure white in color. These dogs have a wedge-shaped head, pointed ears, and a plumed tail not to mention an intelligent expression and a fun-loving personality. The Samoyed is the ideal arctic breed because its thick coat protects it from cold and harsh weather while its white color allows it to blend in with its surroundings.

You probably won't be surprised to learn that the Samoyed hails from western Siberia and northwest Russia. This breed was developed by the Samoyedic peoples, a nomadic tribe who kept reindeer, using the Samoyed dog to herd them. This breed is a medium-sized dog, generally standing 19 to 23.5 inches (48 to 60 cm) tall and weighing 50 to 60 pounds (23 to 27 kg) at maturity. Many people say, however, that the breed looks larger than it is because of its thick coat that stands out from the body. These dogs have black or dark brown eyes and noses.

The Samoyed is nothing if not a friendly, happy breed and he has boundless energy. While this makes the Sammy a great dog to be around, it also makes him somewhat of a challenge to keep. Unless you are able to provide for your dog's high exercise needs as well as his need for mental stimulation, the Samoyed may not be the right dog for you. It is also important to realize that these dogs were developed as herding dogs which means that they are trained to operate independently. Many herding breeds have a somewhat strong-willed temperament and they can sometimes be tricky to train due to that fact. With time and consistency, however, positive reinforcement training methods generally work well with the Samoyed.

In terms of its benefits as a household pet, the Samoyed is a fairly adaptable breed as long as it gets enough exercise. These dogs are highly affectionate and they form strong bonds with family – they also get along very well with children and they can be amenable to cats if they are raised with them. Samoyed dogs have a tendency to bark a lot which makes them good watch dogs and they generally warm up to new people fairly quickly. This dog does have strong territorial tendencies, however, so plenty of socialization is recommended from an early age.

One of the biggest challenges with keeping the Samoyed breed is caring for his thick coat. These dogs shed a lot so you will need to brush your dog on a daily basis. The Samoyed blows his coat once or twice a year as well, so you may need to do some extra brushing during this type. Some people say that the Samoyed is a hypoallergenic breed because its coat produces less dander than other breeds, but most people find that the amount of shedding makes this breed a poor choice for allergy sufferers.

For the most part, the Samoyed is a fairly healthy breed with an average lifespan of 12 to 14 years. Though the Samoyed is sometimes considered a primitive dog breed it unfortunately comes from a fairly limited gene pool which means that it has a high risk for certain genetic disorders. One disease that tends to be hereditary in Samoyed dogs is glomerulopathy, a type of renal disease. Other health problems that may affect the Samoyed breed include diabetes, progressive retinal atrophy, pulmonary stenosis, hip dysplasia, sebaceous adenitis and hypothyroidism. The Samoyed Club of America sets strict standards for DNA testing when it comes to breeding the Samoyed to help prevent the passing of genetic problems.

Summary Samoyed Facts

Pedigree: Spitz-type breed developed by the Samoyedic peoples of Siberia for herding reindeer and pulling sleds

AKC Group: Working Group

Breed Size: medium

Height: 19 to 23.5 inches (48 to 60 cm)

Weight: 50 to 60 lbs. (23 to 27 kg)

Coat Length: medium-long; males have a ruff on the neck

Coat Texture: double coat; dense undercoat, long and coarse outer coat; stands away from the body

Shedding: heavy, frequent grooming needed; blows the coat once or twice a year

Color: solid white tipped with silver

Eyes and Nose: black or dark brown

Ears: small and pointed; prick ears

Tail: plumed and carried over the back

Temperament: sweet, affectionate, lively, playful, loyal, intelligent, trainable

Strangers: may bark at strangers but warms up quickly

Children: very good with children

Other Dogs: generally good with other dogs if properly trained and socialized

Training: intelligent and generally very trainable with time and consistency; positive reinforcement training is best

Exercise Needs: very active and energetic; 30-minute daily walk required with active playtime; may also appreciate training for work or dog sports

Health Conditions: hereditary glomerulopathy, diabetes, progressive retinal atrophy, pulmonary stenosis, hip dysplasia, sebaceous adenitis and hypothyroidism

Lifespan: average 12 to 14 years

Samoyed Breed History

The Samoyed dog breed is named after the Samoyedic peoples, a nomadic tribe native to northwestern Siberia. The Samoyedic people developed the Samoyed dog breed to herd reindeer and to pull sleds when they moved from one location to another. Samoyeds were bred for their thick double coats in order to keep them protected from the harsh Siberian weather and for their love and trust of mankind which makes them excellent companion pets in addition to talented and hard-working dogs.

At the end of the 19th century, the Samoyed breed was brought out of Siberia and used to pull sledges on Arctic and Antarctic expeditions during the early 20th century. Most of the modern Samoyed dogs that were brought to England and the United States are descended from these expedition sled dogs. The first Samoyed registered with the AKC was a Russian import – this registration occurred in 1906. Today, the Samoyed is recognized by the AKC, The Kennel Club, the FCI and a number of other national clubs.

Chapter Two: Things to Know Before Getting a Samoyed

By now you should have a better understanding of what the Samoyed dog is like and what makes this breed so unique. Learning the basic facts about the Samoyed breed is not enough, however, to make a truly educated decision in regards to whether or not this is the right breed for you. In this chapter you will find a collection of practical tips and important information to consider before you make your choice. Here you will find information about licensing your dog, about keeping Samoyeds with other pets, and an overview of the costs for keeping a dog.

Do You Need a License?

Before purchasing a Samoyed dog, you should learn about local licensing requirements that may affect you. The licensing requirements for dog owners vary from one country to another so you may need to do a little bit of research on your own to determine whether you need a dog license or not. In the United States, there are no federal requirements for dog licensing – it is determined at the state level. While some states do not, most states require dog owners to license their dogs on an annual basis.

When you apply for a dog license you will have to submit proof that your dog has been given a rabies vaccine. Dog licenses in the United States cost about $25 (£16.25) per year and they can be renewed annually when you renew your dog's rabies vaccine. Even if your state doesn't require you to license your dog it is still a good idea because it will help someone to identify him if he gets lost so they can return him to you.

In the United Kingdom, licensing requirements for dog owners are a little bit different. The U.K. requires that all dog owners license their dogs and the license can be renewed every twelve months. The cost to license your dog in the U.K. is similar to the U.S. but you do not have to have your dog vaccinated against rabies. In fact, rabies does not exist in the U.K. because it was eradicated through careful control measures. If you travel with your dog to or from the U.K., you will have to obtain a special animal moving license and your dog may have to undergo a period of quarantine to make sure he doesn't carry disease into the country.

Do Samoyeds Get Along with Other Pets?

The Samoyed was developed as a herding breed but they are primarily used for herding reindeer, not smaller animals. This being the case, Samoyed dogs generally do not have a problem with cats and small household pets as long as they are raised together from a young age. Samoyed generally get along with other dogs as well, though they can be a little territorial at times. This is one of the many reasons why early socialization and training is so important. Supervision is also recommended for interactions between your Samoyed and other pets.

How Many Samoyeds Should You Keep?

The Samoyed is a very friendly and gentle breed that tends to form strong bonds with family. Because the Samoyed is a herding breed, however, these dogs can develop a bit of an independent streak. This breed is not recommended if you spend a great deal of time away from home because these dogs do not do well when left alone for long periods of time. Getting a second dog to keep your Samoyed company may not be enough because these dogs require a great deal of physical as well as mental stimulation to control problem behaviors and to meet their exercise requirements each day.

How Much Does it Cost to Keep a Samoyed?

Becoming a dog owner is not cheap. Not only do you have to cover the cost of your Samoyed puppy and any initial supplies you need, but you also have to think about recurring monthly costs for food, veterinary care, and other basic necessities. Unless you are able to cover the cost to keep a dog and meet all of his needs, you should consider another type of pet. In this section you will receive an overview of the initial costs and monthly costs to keep a Samoyed so you can decide whether or not you really can financially support a dog.

Initial Costs

The initial costs for keeping a Samoyed include those costs that you must cover before you can bring your dog home Some of the initial costs you will need to cover include your dog's crate, food/water bowls, toys and accessories, microchipping, initial vaccinations, spay/neuter surgery and supplies for grooming and nail clipping – it also includes the cost of the dog itself. <u>You will find an overview of each of these costs as well as an estimate for each cost on the following page</u>:

Purchase Price – The cost to purchase a Samoyed can vary greatly depending where you find the dog. You can adopt a rescue dog for as little as $200 (£180) but purchasing a puppy - especially a purebred puppy from an AKC-registered breeder - could be much costlier. The cost of a show-quality Samoyed puppy could cost as much as $2,000 (£1,800) or more. For a pet-quality puppy of good breeding, however, the average cost is somewhere between $750 and $1,200 (£675 - £1,080).

Crate – Because the Samoyed is a medium-sized breed that grows up to 60 pounds (27 kg) you may need to purchase a small crate for your puppy and then a larger one once he reaches his adult size. The average cost for a small dog crate is about $30 (£19.50) in most cases.

Food/Water Bowls – In addition to providing your Samoyed with a crate to sleep in, you should also make sure he has a set of high-quality food and water bowls. The best materials for these is stainless steel because it is easy to clean and doesn't harbor bacteria – ceramic is another good option. The average cost for a quality set of stainless steel bowls is about $20 (£18).

Toys – Giving your Samoyed plenty of toys to play with will help to keep him from chewing on things that are not toys – they can also be used to provide mental stimulation and enrichment. To start out, plan to buy an assortment of toys for your dog until you learn what kind he prefers. Be sure to include some rope toys, balls, chew toys, and interactive/puzzle toys. You may want to budget a cost of $50 (£45) for toys just to be sure you have enough to last through the puppy phase.

Microchipping – In the United States and United Kingdom there are no federal or state requirements saying that you have to have your dog microchipped, but it is a very good idea. Your Samoyed could slip out of his collar on a walk or lose his ID tag. If someone finds him without identification, they can take him to a shelter to have his microchip scanned. A microchip is something that is implanted under your dog's skin and it carries a number that is linked to your contact information. The procedure takes just a few minutes to perform and it only costs about $30 (£19.50) in most cases.

Initial Vaccinations – During your puppy's first year of life, he will require a number of different vaccinations. If you purchase your puppy from a reputable breeder, he might already have had a few but you'll still need more over the next few months as well as booster shots each year. You should budget about $50 (£32.50) for initial vaccinations.

Spay/Neuter Surgery – If you don't plan to breed your Samoyed you should have him or her neutered or spayed before 6 months of age. The cost for this surgery will vary depending where you go and on the sex of your dog. If you go to a veterinary surgeon, the cost for spay/neuter surgery could be very high but you can save money by going to a veterinary clinic. The average cost for neuter surgery is $50 to $100 (£32.50 - £65) and spay surgery costs about $100 to $200 (£65 - £130).

Supplies/Accessories – In addition to purchasing your Samoyed's crate and food/water bowls, you should also purchase some basic grooming supplies (several brushes and a wide-toothed comb) as well as a leash and collar. The cost for these items will vary depending on the quality, but you should budget about $100 (£32.50) for these extra costs.

Initial Costs for Samoyeds		
Cost	**One Dog**	**Two Dogs**
Purchase Price	$200 - $2,000 (£180 - £1,800)	$400 - $4,000 (£360 - £3,600)
Crate	$30 (£19.50)	$60 (£39)
Food/Water Bowl	$20 (£18)	$40 (£36)
Toys	$50 (£45)	$100 (£90)
Microchipping	$30 (£19.50)	$60 (£39)
Vaccinations	$50 (£32.50)	$100 (£65)
Spay/Neuter	$50 to $200 (£32.50 - £130)	$100 to $400 (£65 - £260)
Accessories	$100 (£90)	$100 (£90)
Total	$530 to $2,480 (£477 – £2,232)	$960 to $4,860 (£864 – £4,374)

*Costs may vary depending on location
**U.K. prices based on an estimated exchange of $1 = £0.90

Monthly Costs

The monthly costs for keeping a Samoyed as a pet include those costs which recur on a monthly basis. The most important monthly cost for keeping a dog is, of course, food. In addition to food, however, you'll also need to think about things like grooming costs, annual license renewal, toy replacements, and veterinary exams. You will find an overview of each of these costs as well as an estimate for each cost below:

Food and Treats – Feeding your Samoyed a healthy diet is very important for his health and wellness. A high-quality diet for dogs is not cheap, so you should be prepared to spend around $35 (£31.50) on a large bag of high-quality dog food which will last you at least a month. You should also include a monthly budget of about $10 (£6.50) for treats.

Grooming Costs – One of the biggest recurring expenses you will have for a Samoyed is grooming costs – you can save money, however, by brushing and grooming your dog yourself. The average cost for a visit to the groomer is about $50 and if you don't plan to groom your dog yourself you should plan to have him professionally groomed every 6 to 8 weeks. If you take an average of 6 annual visits and divide the cost evenly over 12 months you get an average cost around $25 (£22.50) per month.

License Renewal – The cost to license your Samoyed will generally be about $25 (£16.25) and you can renew the license for the same price each year. License renewal cost divided over 12 months is about $2 (£1.30) per month.

Veterinary Exams – In order to keep your Samoyed healthy, you should take him to the veterinarian about every six months after he passes puppyhood. You might have to take him more often for the first 12 months to make sure he gets his vaccines on time. The average cost for a vet visit is about $40 (£26) so, if you have two visits per year, it averages to about $7 (£4.55) per month.

Other Costs – In addition to the monthly costs for your Samoyed's food, grooming, license renewal, and vet visits there are also some other cost you might have to pay occasionally. These costs might include things like replacements for worn-out toys, a larger collar as your puppy grows, cleaning products, and more. You should budget about $15 (£9.75) per month for extra costs.

Monthly Costs for Samoyeds		
Cost	**One Dog**	**Two Dogs**
Food and Treats	$45 (£40.50)	$90 (£81)
Grooming Costs	$25 (£22.50)	$50 (£45)
License Renewal	$2 (£1.30)	$4 (£3.60)
Veterinary Exams	$7 (£4.55)	$14 (£12.60)
Other Costs	$15 (£9.75)	$30 (£19.50)
Total	$94 (£85)	$188 (£170)

*Costs may vary depending on location

**U.K. prices based on an estimated exchange of $1 = £0.90

What are the Pros and Cons of Samoyeds?

As wonderful as the Samoyed breed is, it is definitely not the right breed for everyone. This breed has a lot of energy and its coat sheds quite a bit so you should be prepared to put a lot of time into caring for your Samoyed dog. To give you a better idea of what the good and bad things are about this breed, consult the list of pros and cons below. You will find a list of pros and cons for the Samoyed dog breed listed below:

Pros for the Samoyed Breed

- The Samoyed has a beautiful white coat with a lovely silvery sheen – it is quite unique.

- Samoyeds are very friendly and gentle dogs – they get along well with children and make friends quickly.
- The Samoyed is an adaptable breed as long as its needs for exercise are met each day.
- Samoyeds are a medium-sized breed, though some grow larger than others.
- The Samoyed is a very intelligent breed that responds well to training and is compatible with various dog sports and activities.

Cons for the Samoyed Breed

- The Samoyed's double coat sheds a lot and it needs to be brushed on a daily basis.
- Samoyed dogs are very high energy and they need a lot of mental stimulation as well as physical exercise.
- Samoyeds have a tendency to bark, though this can be controlled with proper training.
- The Samoyed breed is prone to a number of genetic conditions so careful breeding is absolutely essential.
- Samoyeds can become destructive when they get bored if left alone for too long.
- The breed has a bit of a stubborn side due to its herding heritage – this can be controlled with training.

Chapter Three: Purchasing Samoyed Dogs

Having learned the basics about the Samoyed breed as well as some of the practical information about keeping these dogs as pets, you may have a better idea whether or not this is the right breed for you. If it is you may be eager to learn where to find a Samoyed puppy. In this chapter you will receive some helpful tips for picking out a Samoyed puppy and for puppy-proofing your home. You will also receive tips for choosing a reputable breeder which is very important for the Samoyed breed because they are prone to a number of serious genetic health defects.

Where Can You Buy Samoyed Puppies?

If you are sure that a Samoyed breed is right for you, you need to start thinking about where you are going to get your new dog. Many people think that the best place to find a dog is at the pet store but, unfortunately, they are greatly mistaken. While the puppies at the pet store might look cute and cuddly, there is no way to know whether they are actually healthy or well-bred. Many pet stores get their puppies from puppy mills and they sell the puppies to unsuspecting dog lovers. Puppy mill puppies are often already sick by the time they make it to the pet store, often traveling across state lines to get there.

A puppy mill is a type of breeding facility that focuses on breeding and profit more than the health and wellbeing of the dogs. Puppy mills usually keep their dogs in squalid conditions, forcing them to bear litter after litter of puppies with little to no rest in between. Many of the breeders used in puppy mills are poorly bred themselves or unhealthy to begin with which just ensures that the puppies will have the same problems. The only time you should bring home a puppy from a pet store is if the store has a partnership with a local shelter and that is where they get their dogs. If the pet store can't tell you which breeder the puppies came from, or if they don't offer you any paperwork or registration for the puppy, it is likely that the puppy came from a puppy mill.

Rather than purchasing a Samoyed puppy from a pet store, your best bet is to find a reputable Cocker Spaniel breeder – preferably and AKC-registered breeder in the United States or a Kennel Club-registered breeder in the U.K. If you visit the website for either of these organizations, you can find a list of breeders for all of the club-recognized breeds. You can also look for breeders on the website for other breed clubs like the Samoyed Club of America or the British Samoyed Club. Even if these organizations don't provide a list of breeders you may be able to speak with members to find information.

If you don't have your heart set on a Samoyed puppy, consider adopting a rescue from a local shelter. There are many benefits associated with rescuing an adult dog. For one thing, adoption fees are generally under $200 (£180) which is much more affordable than the $800 to $1,200 (£720 to £1,080) fee to buy a puppy from a breeder. Plus, an adult dog will already be housetrained and may have some obedience training as well. As an added bonus, most shelters spay/neuter their dogs before adopting them out so you won't have to pay for the surgery yourself. Another benefit is that an adult dog has already surpassed the puppy stage so his personality is set – with a puppy you can never quite be sure how your puppy will turn out.

If you are thinking about adopting a Samoyed, consider one of these breed-specific rescues:

United States Rescues:

National Samoyed Rescue.
<http://www.samoyedrescue.org/>

Samoyed Rescue.
<http://www.samoyed.org/samrescue.html>

MidAtlantic Samoyed Rescue.
<http://www.samrescue.com/>

Samoyed Rescue Alliance.
<http://www.samoyedrescue.com/>

Potomac Valley Samoyed Club.
<http://www.potomacvalleysams.com/Samoyed_Rescue.html>

You can also find a list of Samoyed rescue groups on the Samoyed Club of America website:
<http://www.samoyedclubofamerica.org/the-samoyed/choosing-a-dog/rescue-groups/>

United Kingdom Rescues:

Samoyed Association Rescue.

<http://www.samoyedrescue.co.uk/>

Samoyed Rescue Society.

<http://monakmore.co.uk/samoyedrescue/>

White Samoyed Rescue.

<http://whitesamoyed.co.uk/rescue/>

You can also find a list of Samoyed rescues in the U.K. on The Kennel Club website:

<http://www.thekennelclub.org.uk/services/public/findarescue/Default.aspx?breed=5139>

How to Choose a Reputable Samoyed Breeder

As it has already been mentioned, the Samoyed breed is susceptible to a number of genetic health defects. This being the case, you need to be extremely careful about where you get your puppy. A reputable breeder will perform thorough DNA testing on his breeding stock to ensure that these genetic conditions are not passed down. It is your job to find one of these breeders when you are ready to purchase a Samoyed puppy.

When you are ready to start looking for a Samoyed puppy you may begin your search for a breeder online. A simple internet search will probably give you a variety of results but, if you want to find a reputable breeder, you may have to dig a little deeper. Compile a list of breeders from whatever sources you can and then take the time to go through each option to determine whether the breeder is reputable and responsible or not. You do not want to run the risk of purchasing a puppy from a hobby breeder or from one who doesn't follow responsible breeding practices.

Once you have your list of breeders on hand you can go through them one-by-one to narrow down your options. Go through the following steps to do so:

- Visit the website for each breeder on your list (if they have one) and look for key information about the breeder's history and experience.

- o Check for club registrations and a license, if applicable.
- o If the website doesn't provide any information about the facilities or the breeder you are best just moving on.
- After ruling out some of the breeders, contact the remaining breeders on your list by phone
  - o Ask the breeder questions about his experience with breeding dogs in general and about the Samoyed breed in particular.
  - o Ask for information about the breeding stock including registration numbers and health information.
  - o Expect a reputable breeder to ask you questions about yourself as well – a responsible breeder wants to make sure that his puppies go to good homes.
- Schedule an appointment to visit the facilities for the remaining breeders on your list after you've weeded a few more of them out.
  - o Ask for a tour of the facilities, including the place where the breeding stock is kept as well as the facilities housing the puppies.
  - o If things look unorganized or unclean, do not purchase from the breeder.

- o Make sure the breeding stock is in good condition and that the puppies are all healthy-looking and active.
- Narrow down your list to a final few options and then interact with the puppies to make your decision.
  - o Make sure the breeder provides some kind of health guarantee and ask about any vaccinations the puppies may have already received.
- Put down a deposit, if needed, to reserve a puppy if they aren't ready to come home yet.

Tips for Selecting a Healthy Samoyed Puppy

After you have narrowed down your options for Samoyed breeders you then need to pick out your puppy. If you are a first-time dog owner, do not let yourself become caught up in the excitement of a new puppy – take the time to make a careful selection. If you rush the process you could end up with a puppy that isn't healthy or one whose personality isn't compatible with your family. Follow the steps below to pick out your Samoyed puppy:

- Ask the breeder to give you a tour of the facilities, especially where the puppies are kept.
  - o Make sure the facilities where the puppies are housed is clean and sanitary – if there is

evidence of diarrhea, do not purchase one of the puppies because they may already be sick.

- Take a few minutes to observe the litter as a whole, watching how the puppies interact with each other.
  - o The puppies should be active and playful, interacting with each other in a healthy way.
  - o Avoid puppies that appear to be lethargic and those that have difficulty moving – they could be sick.
- Approach the litter and watch how the puppies react to you when you do.
  - o If the puppies appear frightened they may not be properly socialized and you do not want a puppy like that.
  - o The puppies may be somewhat cautious, but they should be curious and interested in you.
- Let the puppies approach you and give them time to sniff and explore you before you interact with them.
  - o Pet the puppies and encourage them to play with a toy, taking the opportunity to observe their personalities.
  - o Single out any of the puppies that you think might be a good fit and spend a little time with them.
- Pick up the puppy and hold him to see how he responds to human contact.

- o The puppy might squirm a little but it shouldn't be frightened of you and it should enjoy being pet.
- Examine the puppy's body for signs of illness and injury
  - o The puppy should have clear, bright eyes with no discharge. The coat should be even and bright white, no patches of hair loss or discoloration.
  - o The ears should be clean and clear with no discharge or inflammation.
  - o The puppy's stomach may be round but it shouldn't be distended or swollen.
  - o The puppy should be able to walk and run normally without any mobility problems.
- Narrow down your options and choose the puppy that you think is the best fit.

Once you've chosen your puppy, ask the breeder about the next steps. Do not take the puppy home if it isn't at least 8 weeks old and unless it has been fully weaned and eating solid food.

Puppy-Proofing Your Home

After you've picked out your Samoyed puppy you may still have to wait a few weeks until you can bring him home. During this time, you should take steps to prepare your home, making it a safe place for your puppy. The process of making your home safe for your puppy is called "puppy proofing" and it involves removing or storing away anything and everything that could harm your puppy. It might help for you to crawl around the house on your hands and knees, viewing things from your puppy's perspective.

<u>On the following page you will find a list of things you should do when you are puppy-proofing your home</u>:

- Make sure your trash and recycling containers have a tight-fitting lid or store them in a cabinet.

- Put away all open food containers and keep them out of reach of your puppy.

- Store cleaning products and other hazardous chemicals in a locked cabinet or pantry where your puppy can't get them.

- Make sure electrical cords and blind pulls are wrapped up and placed out of your puppy's reach.

- Pick up any small objects or toys that could be a choking hazard if your puppy chews on them.

- Cover or drain any open bodies of water such as the toilet, and outdoor pond, etc.

- Store any medications and beauty products in the medicine cabinet out of your puppy's reach.

- Check your home for any plants that might be toxic to dogs and remove them or put them out of reach.

- Block off fire places, windows, and doors so your puppy can't get into trouble.

- Close off any stairwells and block the entry to rooms where you do not want your puppy to be.

Chapter Four: Caring for Samoyed Dogs

Now that you have a better understanding of the Samoyed breed and you know where to get one you may be wondering about the details of keeping Samoyed dogs as pets. Before you truly decide if this is the right breed for you, you should consider the habitat and exercise requirements for these dogs. Samoyeds are by no means a low-maintenance breed so you need to make sure you can meet the breed's exercise requirements in order to keep your dog healthy. You will find this information and more in the following pages of this chapter.

Habitat and Exercise Requirements for Samoyeds

The Samoyed dog is a medium-sized breed so they do not require as much space as some dogs. It is important to consider, however, that this breed is highly active so they do need a lot of daily exercise and, ideally, a fenced outdoor space where they can run and play. If you live in a small condo or an urban apartment without access to outdoor greenspace, the Samoyed is probably not the right breed for you. You also need to take your dog on a 30-minute walk at least once a day to meet his most basic needs for physical exercise. Samoyeds are a fairly adaptable breed but only if their exercise needs are met.

In addition to making sure your Samoyed gets enough exercise, you will also need to provide him with certain things. A crate is one of the most important things you will need when you bring your new Samoyed puppy home. Not only will it be a place for your puppy to sleep, but it will also be a place where you can confine him during the times when you are away from home or when you cannot keep a close eye on him. As your Samoyed grows into his adult size you may need to replace his crate with a bigger one. Ideally, your dog's crate should only be large enough for him to comfortably stand up, sit down, lie down, and turn around in. Your puppy will also need some other basic things like a water bowl, a food bowl, a collar, a leash, toys, and grooming supplies.

When shopping for food and water bowls, safety and sanitation are the top two considerations. Stainless steel is the best material to go with because it is easy to clean and resistant to bacteria. Ceramic is another good option, though it may be a little heavier. Avoid plastic food and water bowls because they can become scratched and the scratches may harbor bacteria. For your dog's collar and leash, choose one that is appropriate to his size. This may mean that you will purchase several collars and leashes while your puppy is still growing. You might also consider a harness – this will be helpful during leash training because it will improve your control over your puppy and it will distribute pressure across his back instead of putting it all on his throat.

Provide your Samoyed puppy with an assortment of different toys and let him figure out which ones he likes. Having a variety of toys around the house is very important because you'll need to use them to redirect your puppy's natural chewing behavior as he learns what he is and is not allowed to chew on. Samoyeds are a very intelligent breed, so you should have some interactive and puzzle toys for your puppy to play with as well. Leaving one of these toys with your puppy when you are away from home will help to reduce the risk for destructive behavior. As for grooming supplies, you'll need a wire-pin brush for daily brushing as well as a slicker brush to work through tangles. You might also want a metal comb with wide teeth that you can use to work through stubborn mats and tangles.

Setting Up Your Puppy's Area

Before you bring your Samoyed puppy home, you should set up a particular area in your home for him to call his own. The ideal setup will include your puppy's crate, a comfy dog bed, his food and water bowls, and an assortment of toys. You can arrange all of these items in a small room that is easy to block off or you can use a puppy playpen to give your puppy some free space while still keeping him somewhat confined.

When you bring your puppy home you'll have to work with him a little bit to get him used to the crate. It is very important that you do this because you do not want your puppy to form a negative association with the crate. You want your puppy to learn that the crate is his own special place, a place where he can go to relax and take a nap if he wants to. If you use the crate as punishment, your puppy will not want to use it.

To get your puppy used to the crate, try tossing a few treats into it and let him go fish them out. Feeding your puppy his meals in the crate with the door open will be helpful as well. You can also incorporate the crate into your playtime, tossing toys into the crate or hiding treats under a blanket in the crate. As your puppy gets used to the crate you can start keeping him in it with the door closed for short periods of time, working your way up to longer periods. Just be sure to let your puppy outside before and after you confine him and never force him to stay in the crate for longer than he is physically capable of holding his bowels and his bladder.

Chapter Five: Meeting Your Samoyed's Nutritional Needs

One of your biggest jobs as a dog owner is to provide your Samoyed with a high-quality and nutritious diet. Unfortunately, achieving this goal is not always as simple as it seems because there are many low-quality dog foods out there that are disguised as quality products. To help you choose the best diet for your dog you will find an overview of your Samoyed's nutritional needs in this chapter as well as some practical information for choosing a high-quality dog food product and for feeding your dog.

The Nutritional Needs of Dogs

Like all mammals, dogs require a balance of the three macronutrients - protein, carbohydrate and fat in their diets – this is in addition to essential vitamins and minerals. It is important to understand, however, that your Samoyed's nutritional needs are very different from your own. For dogs, protein is the most important nutritional consideration followed by fat and then carbohydrates. In order to keep your dog healthy, you need to create a diet that provides the optimal levels of these three macronutrients.

The portion of your dog's diet that comes from protein should be made up of animal sources like meat, poultry, and fish as well as meat meals. Protein is made up of amino acids which are the building blocks that make up your dog's tissues and cells. It also provides some energy for your dog. The most highly concentrated type of energy your Samoyed needs, however, is fat. This nutrient is particularly important for active and working dogs because they burn a lot of energy during the day and therefore very high needs for calories.

In addition to protein and fat, your Samoyed also needs carbohydrates to provide dietary fiber and various vitamins and minerals. Dogs do not have a specific need for carbohydrates but they should always come from digestible sources since a dog's digestive tract is not designed to process plant foods as effectively as protein and fat. Your dog also needs plenty of fresh water on a daily basis as well as key vitamins and minerals.

The exact number of calories your Samoyed needs will vary according to his age, sex, weight, and activity level. As a general rule, smaller dogs have higher calorie needs per pound of bodyweight than large-breed dogs, especially if the breed is very active like the Samoyed. Based on the average adult size for the breed (50 to 60 pounds) you can expect your Samoyed to need about 1,500 calories per day. The more active your dog is, however, the higher is calorie needs are going to be.

How to Select a High-Quality Dog Food Brand

Shopping for dog food can be difficult for some dog owners simply because there are so many different options to choose from. If you walk into your local pet store you will see multiple aisles filled with bags of dog food from different brands and most brands offer a number of different formulas. So how do you choose a healthy dog food for your Samoyed?

The best place to start when shopping for dog food is to read the dog food label. Pet food in the United States is loosely regulated by the American Association of Feed Control Officials (AAFCO) and they evaluate commercial dog food products according to their ability to meet the basic nutritional needs of dogs in various life stages. If the product meets these basic needs, the label will carry some kind of statement from AAFCO like this:

"[Product Name] is formulated to meet the nutritional levels established by the AAFCO Dog Food nutrient profiles for [Life Stage]."

If the dog food product you are looking at contains this statement you can move on to reading the ingredients list. Dog food labels are organized in descending order by volume. This means that the ingredients at the top of the list are used in higher quantities than the ingredients at the end of the list. This being the case, you want to see high-quality sources of animal protein at the beginning of the list. Things like fresh meat, poultry or fish are excellent ingredients but they contain about 80% water. After the product is cooked, the actual volume and protein content of the ingredient will be less. Meat meals (like chicken meal or salmon meal) have already been cooked down so they contain up to 300% more protein by weight than fresh meats.

In addition to high-quality animal proteins, you want to check the ingredients list for digestible carbohydrates and healthy fats. For dogs, digestible carbohydrates include things like brown rice and oatmeal, as long as they have been cooked properly. You can also look for gluten-free and grain-free options like sweet potato and tapioca. It is best to avoid products that are made with corn, wheat, or soy ingredients because they are low in nutritional value and may trigger food allergies in your dog.

In terms of fat, you want to see at least one animal source such as chicken fat or salmon oil. Plant-based fats like flaxseed and canola oil are not necessarily bad, but they are less biologically valuable for your dog. If they are accompanied by an animal source of fat, it is okay. Just make sure that the fats included in the recipe provide a blend of both omega-3 and omega-6 fatty acids. This will help to preserve the quality and condition of your Maltese dog's skin and coat.

In addition to checking the ingredients list for beneficial ingredients you should also know that there are certainly things you do NOT want to see listed. Avoid products made with low-quality fillers like corn gluten meal or rice bran – you should also avoid artificial colors, flavors, and preservatives. Some commonly used artificial preservatives are BHA and BHT. In most cases the label will tell you if natural preservatives are used.

Tips for Feeding Your Samoyed

The Samoyed is a medium-sized breed but most commercial dog food manufacturers do not offer size-specific formulas for medium-sized dogs. Because the Samoyed is also a high-energy working breed, however, an active or working breed formula might be a good fit. These recipes are typically made with high levels of protein to maintain lean muscle mass and higher levels of fat to provide additional calories and energy. If you choose an active dog formula for your Samoyed just be sure that it is made with quality ingredients.

Once you've chosen a healthy diet for your Samoyed dog you need to know how much and how often to feed him. Because different dog food products have different calorie content you should follow the feeding instructions on the label as a starting point. Most dog food labels provide feeding instructions by weight, so make sure you know how much your dog weighs. It is also important to remember that these are feeding suggestions – you might have to alter the ration for your dog. If your Samoyed starts to gain too much weight, decrease his daily ration a little. If he loses weight or becomes lethargic, increase it a little bit.

In addition to knowing how much to feed your Samoyed you also need to think about how often to feed him. Most dog owners recommend feeding your dog twice a day. When your Samoyed is a puppy, however, he will need more food to fuel his growth so you should allow him to eat as much as he wants. Once he reaches full size, though, you may want to start rationing his food. Keep track of your dog's weight and keep an eye on his body condition – consult your veterinarian if you have concerns about your Samoyed's weight or energy levels.

Dangerous Foods to Avoid

It might be tempting to give in to your Samoyed when he is begging at the table, but certain "people foods" can actually be toxic for your dog. As a general rule, you should never feed your dog anything unless you are 100% sure that it is safe. <u>Below you will find a list of foods that can be toxic to dogs and should therefore be avoided</u>:

- Alcohol
- Apple seeds
- Avocado
- Cherry pits
- Chocolate
- Coffee
- Garlic
- Grapes/raisins
- Hops
- Macadamia nuts
- Mold
- Mushrooms
- Mustard seeds
- Onions/leeks
- Peach pits
- Potato leaves/stems
- Rhubarb leaves
- Tea
- Tomato leaves/stems
- Walnuts
- Xylitol
- Yeast dough

If your Samoyed eats any of these foods, contact the Pet Poison Control hotline right away at (888) 426 – 4435.

Chapter Six: Training Your Samoyed

Aside from providing your Samoyed with a healthy diet, one of your most important tasks as a dog owner is to train your dog. Dog training is not as complicated as many people assume it is, but it does take a certain degree of dedication and a lot of treats. The more often you work with your Samoyed puppy the faster he will learn. In this chapter you will receive some tips for socializing your new Samoyed puppy to ensure that your dog grows up to be a well-adjusted adult dog. You will also receive some general tips for positive reinforcement training and a guide for crate training your dog.

Socializing Your New Samoyed Puppy

It is important to realize that your Samoyed puppy will be the most impressionable during the first three months of life. This is when you need to socialize him because the experiences he has as a puppy will shape the way he interacts with the world as an adult. If you don't properly socialize your Samoyed puppy, he could grow up to be a mal-adjusted adult who fears new experiences. Fortunately, socialization is very simple – all you have to do is make sure that your puppy has plenty of new experiences. <u>Below you will find a list of things you should expose your puppy to for properly socialization</u>:

- Introduce your puppy to friends in the comfort of your own home.

- Invite friends with dogs or puppies to come meet your Samoyed (make sure everyone is vaccinated).

- Expose your puppy to people of different sizes, shapes, gender, and skin color.

- Introduce your puppy to children of different ages – just make sure they know how to handle the puppy safely.

- Take your puppy with you in the car when you run errands.

- Walk your puppy in as many places as possible so he is exposed to different surfaces and surroundings.

- Expose your puppy to water from hoses, sprinklers, showers, pools, etc.

- Make sure your puppy experiences loud noises such as fireworks, cars backfiring, loud music, thunder, etc.

- Introduce your puppy to various appliances and tools such as blenders, lawn mowers, vacuums, etc.

- Walk your puppy with different types of harnesses, collars, and leashes.

- Once he is old enough, take your puppy to the dog park to interact with other dogs.

Positive Reinforcement for Obedience Training

Many people assume that dog training is difficult or complicated but it is actually quite simple – it all has to do with the rewards. Think about this: if you want someone do so something for you, you probably offer them something in return. The same concept is true for dog training – if you reward your dog for performing a particular behavior then he will be more likely to repeat it in the future. This is called positive reinforcement training and it is one of the simplest yet most effective training methods you can use as a Samoyed dog owner.

The key to success with dog training is two-fold. For one thing, you need to make sure that your dog understands what it is you are asking him. If he doesn't know what a command means it doesn't matter how many times you say it, he won't respond correctly. In order to teach your dog what a command means you should give it and then guide him to perform the behavior. Once he does, immediately give him a treat and praise him – the sooner you reward after identifying the desired behavior, the faster your puppy will learn.

The second key to success in dog training is consistency. While your puppy is learning basic obedience commands you need to use the same commands each and every time and you need to be consistent in rewarding him. If you maintain consistency it should only take a few repetitions for your puppy to learn what you expect of him. You can then move on to another command and alternate between them to reinforce your puppy's understanding. Just be sure to keep your training sessions short – about 15 minutes – so your puppy doesn't get bored.

Crate Training - Housebreaking Your Puppy

In addition to obedience training, house training is very important for puppies. After all, you don't want to spend your dog's entirely life following after him with a pooper scooper. The key to house training is to use your puppy's crate appropriately. When you are able to watch your puppy, keep him in the same room with you at all times and take him outdoors once every hour or so to give him a chance to do his business. Always lead him to a particular section of the yard and give him a command like "Go pee" so he learns what is expected of him when you take him to this area.

When you can't watch your puppy and overnight you should confine him to his crate. The crate should be just large enough for your puppy to stand up, sit down, turn around and lie down in. Keeping it this size will ensure that he views the crate as his den and he will be reluctant to soil it. Just make sure that you don't keep your puppy in the crate for longer than he is physically capable of holding his bladder. Always take your puppy out before putting him in the crate and immediately after releasing him.

If you give your puppy ample opportunity to do his business outdoors and you keep him confined to the crate when you can't watch him, housetraining should only take a few weeks. Again, consistency is key here so always reward and praise your puppy for doing his business outside so he learns to do it that way. If your puppy does have an accident, do not punish him because he will not understand – he won't associate the punishment with the crime so he will just learn to fear you instead.

Chapter Seven: Grooming Your Samoyed

One of the things that makes the Samoyed breed so beautiful is his plush white coat. Though the Samoyed's coat is absolutely gorgeous, it definitely isn't low-maintenance. You need to brush your dog's coat daily to prevent mats and to help distribute the natural oils produced by his skin – these oils help to moisturize your dog's skin and keep his coat shiny and soft. In this chapter you will receive some helpful tips for grooming your Samoyed including a list of recommended supplies and instructions for various grooming tasks.

Recommended Tools to Have on Hand

If you plan to groom your Samoyed yourself, you will need certain tools and supplies. Even if you choose to have your dog professionally groomed, you should still have some supplies available for daily brushing and occasional bathing. <u>You will find a list of several recommended grooming tools and supplies below</u>:

- Wire-pin brush
- Metal wide-tooth comb
- Slicker brush (or undercoat rake)
- Small, sharp scissors
- Dog-friendly shampoo
- Nail clippers
- Dog-friendly ear cleaning solution
- Dog toothbrush
- Dog-friendly toothpaste

Learning how to groom your Samoyed properly will take some time but it will be much easier if you have the right tools on hand. Don't be afraid to take your dog to a professional groomer and ask them to show you how to groom your dog properly.

Tips for Bathing and Grooming Samoyeds

The Samoyed's coat is very thick and plush which means that it sheds quite a bit. To help keep your dog's shedding under control, you should plan to brush your dog every day or, at the very least, a few times a week. Keep in mind that double-coated breeds like the Samoyed also blow their coats once or twice a year so you may need to do some extra grooming during that time.

Brushing your Samoyed's coat is very easy if you know how to do it properly but it will take some time– just start at the base of the neck and work your way along the dog's back, down his legs, and under his belly. Always brush in the direction of hair growth and move slowly so you don't hurt your dog if you come across a snag. The more frequently you brush your dog, the healthier his coat will be and the fewer mats and tangles he will develop.

If you encounter a mat or a tangle while brushing your Samoyed, try using a wide-toothed comb to gently work through it. If you can't work the tangle out, you may need to cut it out of your dog's coat. Take a pair of sharp scissors in one hand and pinch the hair at the base of the mat (between the dog's skin and the mat) with your other hand – cut through the hairs a few at a time while gently pulling on the mat until it comes free. If your dog's coat is severely matted, you may want to consult a professional groomer. You should not, however, have your Samoyed's coat trimmed or clipped under any circumstances. The only exception is to perhaps trim the fur between the feet to prevent mats.

If you need to bathe your Samoyed, you will want to brush him first. When you are ready for the bath, fill the bathtub with a few inches of warm (not hot) water and place your dog inside. Use a cup to pour water over your dog's back or use a handheld sprayer to wet down his coat. Once your dog's coat is dampened, apply a small amount of dog-friendly shampoo and work it into a lather. After shampooing, rinse your dog's coat thoroughly to get rid of all the soap and then towel him dry. If it is warm you might be able to let his coat air-dry but if it is cold in your house, you should finish it off with a blow dryer on the lowest possible heat setting.

Other Grooming Tasks

In addition to brushing and bathing your Samoyed, you also need to engage in some other grooming tasks including trimming your dog's nails, cleaning his ears, and brushing his teeth. These tasks are not complicated, nor do they take a lot of time to complete, but they are very important for your dog's health and wellbeing. <u>You will find an overview of each of these grooming tasks below</u>:

Trimming Your Dog's Nails

Your Samoyed's nails grow in the same way that your own nails grow so they need to be trimmed occasionally. Most down owners find that trimming their dog's nails once a week or twice a month is sufficient. Before you trim your dog's nails for the first time you should have your veterinarian or a professional groomer show you how to do it. A dog's nail contains a quick – the blood vessel that supplies blood to the nail – and if you cut the nail too short you could sever it. A severed quick will cause your dog pain and it will bleed profusely. The best way to avoid cutting your dog's nails too short is to just trim the sharp tip on a weekly basis or as needed.

Cleaning Your Dog's Ears

The Samoyed has prick ears which means that they stand upright instead of hanging down on either side of his head. Dogs with prick ears have a lower risk for ear infections than dogs with drop ears (ears that hang down) because their ears get more air circulation which helps to keep them dry. Wet ears become a breeding ground for bacteria and yeast which can cause ear infections.

Even though Samoyeds have a lower risk for ear infections that other breeds, you still need to keep your dog's ears clean and dry. If you have to clean your dog's ears, use a dog ear cleaning solution and squeeze a few drops into the ear canal. Then, massage the base of your dog's ears to distribute the solution then wipe it away using a clean cotton ball.

Brushing Your Dog's Teeth

Brushing your Samoyed's teeth may seem silly but neglecting your dog's dental health which is a serious mistake. Dogs are just as much at risk for dental problems as humans are and, if left untreated, dental problems can lead to serious infections or bone loss. You should brush your dog's teeth with a dog-friendly toothbrush and dog toothpaste to preserve his dental health. Feeing your dog dental treats and giving him hard rubber toys can also help to maintain his dental health.

Chapter Eight: Breeding Samoyeds

The only thing better than one Samoyed puppy is a whole litter of puppies! At least, that is the way many people think. What you may not realize is that breeding Samoyeds (or any dog) is a big responsibility. Not only do you need to make sure that your breeding pair are genetically sound and compatible but you also need to cover some significant financial investments in the health and wellness of your female dog and her puppies. You should not breed your Samoyed without doing a lot of research first – the information in this chapter is intended to provide you with general information about Samoyed breeding only.

Basic Dog Breeding Information

Before you decide whether or not to breed your Samoyed, you should take the time to learn the basics about dog breeding in general. If you do not want to breed your dog, the ASPCA recommends having him neutered or her spayed before the age of 6 months. For female dogs, six months is around the time the dog experiences her first heat. Heat is just another name for the estrus cycle in dogs and it generally lasts for about 14 to 21 days. The frequency of heat may vary slightly from one dog to another but it generally occurs twice a year. When your female dog goes into heat, this is when she is capable of becoming pregnant.

If you do plan to breed your Samoyed, it is important that you wait until she reaches sexual maturity. Your dog may be full-size by the time she reaches one year of age, but most dog breeders recommend waiting until she is 18 months to two years old to breed her. Not only does this ensure that the dog is mature enough to physically carry and bear a litter, but it also provides enough time for any serious health problems to develop. If the dog does display signs of congenital health problems, she should not be bred for fear of passing them on. It is also important not to breed your Cocker Spaniel after the age of 8 for her own safety.

In addition to making sure that your Samoyed are the right age for breeding, you also have to be careful about choosing the right pairing. You should only breed dogs if your goal is to preserve or improve the breed – it should not be done for selfish reasons such as to make money. If you do breed these dogs, you need to make sure that both the male and female are good examples of the breed standard and that you breed them in such a way as to preserve that standard. The Samoyed Club of America provides some detailed information about the details and risks involved in dog breeding – if you are seriously considering breeding your Samoyed, review these things very carefully to ensure that you are making a smart decision. Here is a link to the breeding recommendations for Samoyeds:

<http://www.samoyedclubofamerica.org/the-samoyed/
in-depth/breeding-your-samoyed/>

Once you've made sure that you have chosen the ideal breeding pair you can start to think about the details of heat and breeding. When a female dog goes into heat there are a few common signs you can look for. The first sign of heat is swelling of the vulva – this may be accompanied by a bloody discharge. Over the course of the heat cycle the discharge lightens in color and becomes waterier. By the 10th day of the cycle the discharge is light pink – this is when she begins to ovulate and it is when she is most fertile. If you plan to breed your Samoyed, this is when you want to introduce her to the male dog. If the isn't receptive to the male's advances, wait a day or two before trying again.

A Samoyed is technically capable of conceiving at any point during the heat cycle because the male's sperm can survive in her reproductive tract for up to 5 days. If you don't plan to breed your Samoyed, you need to keep her locked away while she is in heat. A male dog can smell a female dog in heat from several miles away and an intact male dog will go to great lengths to breed. Never take a female dog in heat to the dog park and be very careful about taking her outside at all. Do not leave her unattended in your backyard because a stray dog could get in and breed with her.

If you want to breed your Samoyed, you will need to keep track of her estrus cycle so you know when to breed her. It generally takes a few years for a dog's cycle to become regular and some small-breed dogs go into heat more than twice per year. Keep track of your dog's cycle on a calendar so you know when to breed her. Tracking her cycle and making note of when you introduce her to the male dog will help you predict the due date for the puppies. Once you do start breeding your dog, be sure to skip at least one heat cycle between litters – ideally, you should give your dog a year to rest between litters.

Breeding Tips and Raising Puppies

After the male Samoyed fertilizes the egg inside your female's body, the female will go through the gestation period during which the puppies start to develop inside her womb. The gestation period for Samoyed dogs lasts for anywhere from 61 to 65 days with the average being 63. However, you won't be able to actually tell that your dog is pregnant until after the third week. By the 25th day of pregnancy it is safe for a vet to perform an ultrasound and by day 28 he should be able to feel the puppies by palpating the female's abdomen. At the six week mark an x-ray can be performed to check the size of the litter. The average litter size for Cocker Spaniels is between 4 and 6 puppies, though your dog could have more or less.

While the Samoyed puppies are growing inside your female dog's belly you need to take careful care of her. You don't need to feed your dog any extra until the fourth or fifth week of pregnancy when she really starts to gain weight. Make sure to provide your dog with a healthy diet and keep up with regular vet appointments to make sure the pregnancy is progressing well. Once you reach the fifth week of pregnancy you can increase your dog's daily rations in proportion to her weight gain.

After eight weeks of gestation you should start to get ready for your Samoyed to give birth – in dogs, this is called whelping. You should provide your dog with a clean, safe, and quiet place to give birth such as a large box in a dimly lit room. Line the box with old towels or newspapers for easy cleanup after the birth and make sure your dog has access to the box at all times. As she nears her due date she will start spending more and more time in the box.

When your Samoyed is ready to give birth her internal temperature will decrease slightly. If you want to predict when the puppies will be born you can start taking her internal temperature once a day during the last week of gestation. When the dog's body temperature drops from 100°F to 102°F (37.7°C to 38.8°C to about 98°F (36.6°C), labor is likely to begin very soon. At this point your dog will display obvious signs of discomfort such as pacing, panting, or changing positions. Just let her do her own thing but keep an eye on her in case of complications.

During the early stages of labor, your Samoyed will experience contractions about 10 minutes apart. If she has contractions for more than 2 hours without giving birth, bring her to the vet immediately. Once your Maltese starts whelping, she will whelp one puppy about every thirty minutes. After every puppy is born, she will clean it with her tongue – this will also help stimulate the puppy to start breathing on its own. After all of the puppies have been born, the mother will expel the afterbirth and the puppies will begin nursing.

It is essential that the puppies start nursing as soon as possible after whelping so that they get the colostrum. The colostrum is the first milk a mother produces and it is loaded with nutrients as well as antibodies that will protect the puppies while their own immune systems continue developing. The puppies will generally start nursing on their own or the mother will encourage them. After the puppies nurse for a little while you should make sure that your mother dog eats something as well.

When they are first born, Samoyed puppies are very small – they may only weigh 12 to 17 ounces (340 to 480 grams). Over the next week they will grow to about double their birth weight and they will continue growing over the next several months until they zone in on their adult size. It is a good idea to weigh your Samoyed puppies once a week or so to make sure they are growing at a healthy rate. When Samoyed puppies are born they will have some very fine hair but it isn't enough to keep them warm – your mother dog will help with that. The puppies will be born with their eyes and ears closed but they will start to open around the second or third week following birth.

Your Samoyed puppies will be heavily dependent on their mother for the first few weeks of life until they start becoming more mobile. Most Samoyed puppies start vocalizing and showing social behaviors around 3 weeks of age but they will still spend most of their time with the mother until about week 4. Around 5 to 6 weeks of age you should start offering your puppies small amounts of solid food soaked in broth or water to start the weaning process. Over the next few weeks the puppies will start to nurse less and eat more solid food. Around 8 weeks of age they should be completely weaned – this is when they are ready to be separated from their mother.

Chapter Nine: Showing Your Samoyed

If you are looking for a way to build a stronger bond with your Samoyed, you may want to consider entering him into a dog show. Training and preparing for the show means that you and your dog will get to spend plenty of time together, not to mention sharing the experience of the dog show itself. Before you decide to show your dog, however, you need to make sure that he is a good example of the breed standard. In this chapter you will find an overview of the AKC and The Kennel Club standards for the Samoyed breed as well as some general tips for dog shows.

Samoyed Breed Standards

Before attempting to enter your Samoyed into a dog show you need to make sure that he meets the organization's breed requirements – these requirements are outlined in something called a "breed standard". Essentially, the breed standard is a description of the ideal specimen of the breed and it is the standard to which dogs of that breed are held and judged during the show. Each organization has its own standard for certain breeds so make sure you review the breed standard for the exact show you plan to enter your Samoyed into.

a.) AKC Samoyed Breed Standard

The AKC breed standard for the Samoyed breed provides guidelines for both breeding and showing. AKC-registered breeders must select dogs that adhere to the standards of the breed and all Samoyed owners who seek to show their dogs at AKC shows must compare them to the official breed standard as well.

In the following pages you will find an overview of the breed standard for the Samoyed breed:

General Appearance and Temperament

The dog is a working breed and a picture of beauty, strength and alertness with great dignity and grace. The coat is heavy and weather-resistant with males having more ruff than females. The breed is intelligent and gentle, loyal and eager to serve. The dog is friendly but conservative, not overly aggressive or distrustful.

Head and Neck

The skull is wedge-shaped and broad with a medium-length muzzle. The muzzle tapers toward the nose which is black or dark brown. The ears are strong and erect, slightly rounded at the tips. The eyes are dark and deep-set, almond-shaped with dark eye rims. The neck is strong and well-muscled, carried proud and erect.

Body and Tail

The chest is deep with well sprung ribs but not barrel-chested. The loins are strong and slightly arched, the back straight and medium in length. Females are slightly longer than males. The tail is moderately long, profusely covered with long hair, and carried forward over the back or side when alert, dropped at rest.

Legs and Feet

The upper thighs are well developed, the stifles well bent. The front legs are parallel and straight to the pasterns, flexible with some spring. The feet are large and long, slightly spread but not splayed. Feet turning out, pigeon toes, or cat feet are considered faults. Feathering on the feet is desired but not essential, may be more profuse on females than on males.

Coat and Color

The Samoyed breed is double-coated with the coat standing well away from the body. The undercoat is soft, short and thick, the outer coat longer and harsh, free from curl. The fur forms a ruff around the neck and the coat glistens with a silver sheen. The color should be pure white, white and biscuit, cream, or all biscuit. Any other colors are considered a disqualification.

Size

Adult males should stand 21 to 23.5 inches at the shoulder with females standing 19 to 21 inches tall. The weight should be proportionate to the height.

Gait

The Samoyed trots, it does not pace – he has a quick and agile get with good timing. A choppy or stilted gait is considered a fault.

b.) The Kennel Club Samoyed Breed Standard

The Kennel Club is the main breed registration body in the United Kingdom. This organization recognized the Samoyed breed as part of the Pastoral Group due to its herding abilities. Other breeds belonging to this category include the Border Collie, Finnish Lapphund, Old English Sheepdog, and others. In order to show your Samoyed at a Kennel Club show, he must be a good example of the following breed standard:

General Appearance and Temperament

The Samoyed is a very striking breed, medium in size and well-balanced. The dog is strong, active and graceful – it has great endurance. The breed displays affection to all of mankind with no unprovoked nervousness and aggression is highly undesirable. The expression is intelligent and alert, often a "smiling expression" in the eyes.

Head and Neck

The head is powerful and wedge-shaped with a broad, flat skull and a medium-length muzzle. The lips are black and the nose is preferred black but may be brown or flesh-colored. The hair is short on the head and skull, smooth just before the ears. The neck is strong and arched, the ears slightly rounded at the tips and set well apart. The eyes are almond-shaped and medium to dark brown in color with black eye rims. Light-colored or black eyes are considered undesirable.

Body and Tail

The body is medium in length and broad with an exceptionally strong loin. The chest is deep but not overly broad with well sprung ribs. The tail is long and profusely coated, carried high over the back and to the side when the dog is alert – it may be dropped when at rest. Male dogs should have two normal testicles that are fully descended into the scrotum.

Legs and Feet

The shoulders are well laid, the legs straight and muscular. The hindquarters are very muscular with well angulated stifles. The feet are long and flat, slightly spread, and well feathered. The soles are cushioned with hair. Round cat feet are undesirable.

Coat and Color

The body is covered in a thick, soft undercoat with a harsh but not wiry outer coat that is weather-resistant. The coat stands straight away from the body. The color is pure white, white and biscuit, or cream – the outer coat is tipped in silver.

Size

Adult dogs should measure 51 to 56 cm (20 to 22 inches) at the shoulder and bitches should be 46 to 51 cm (18 to 20 inches) at the shoulder. Weight is proportionate to the height of the dog.

Gait

The dog moves freely with a strong and agile drive, showing great power and elegance.

Preparing Your Samoyed for Show

If you are able to determine that your Samoyed is a good example of the official standard for the breed (according to either the AKC or The Kennel Club), you can then start to think about entering him in a show. Dog shows occur all year-round in many different locations so check the AKC or Kennel Club website for shows in your area. Remember, the rules for each show will be different so make sure to do your research so that you and your Samoyed are properly prepared for the show. On the following page you will find a list of some general and specific rules and regulations to follow during dog show prep:

- Ensure that you've chosen the right show and category for your Samoyed – the AKC and The Kennel Club place the Samoyed in different categories.

- Make sure that your Samoyed is properly socialized to be in an environment with many other dogs and unfamiliar people.

- Ensure that your Samoyed is completely housetrained and able to hold his bladder for at least several hours.

- Solidify your dog's grasp of basic obedience – he should listen and follow basic commands.

- Do some research to learn the requirements for specific shows before you choose one – make sure your dog meets all the requirements for registration.

- Make sure that your Samoyed is caught up on his vaccinations (especially Bordetella since he will be around other dogs) and have your vet clear his overall health for show.

- Have your dog groomed about a week before the show and then take the necessary steps to keep his coat clean and in good condition.

In addition to making sure that your Samoyed meets the requirements for the show and is a good representation of the AKC breed standard, you should also pack a bag of supplies that you will need on the day of show. <u>Below you will find a list of helpful things to include in your dog show supply pack</u>:

- Registration information
- Dog crate or exercise pen
- Grooming table and grooming supplies
- Food and treats
- Food and water bowls
- Trash bags
- Medication (if needed)
- Change of clothes
- Food/water for self
- Paper towels or rags
- Toys for the dog

If you want to show your Samoyed but you don't want to jump immediately into an AKC show, you may be able to find some local dog shows in your area. Local shows may be put on by a branch of the Samoyed Club of America (or another local or regional breed club) and they can be a great place to learn and to connect with other Samoyed dog owners.

Chapter Ten: Keeping Your Samoyed Dog Healthy

Feeding your Samoyed a healthy, high-quality diet is one of the most important things you can do for his long-term health and wellbeing. Even if you are careful about what you feed your dog, however, he could still be exposed to disease. If you take the time to familiarize yourself with some of the conditions most likely to affect the Samoyed breed you will be able to identify the symptoms of they arise and seek proper treatment for your dog.

Common Health Problems Affecting Samoyeds

The Samoyed is a primitive dog breed but it does come from a fairly limited gene pool which means that it has a high risk for certain genetic conditions. The best thing you can do for your Samoyed's health is to learn everything you can about conditions that commonly affect the breed. The more you know, the better you will be able to identify symptoms when they occur. Recognizing the signs of disease is the first step on the road to diagnosis, treatment, and recovery. In this section you will receive an overview of some of the conditions most commonly affecting the Samoyed breed so you know what symptoms to look for and what kind of treatment options are available.

Some of the common conditions affecting Samoyed dogs include the following:

- Cataracts
- Diabetes Mellitus
- Gastric Dilation Volvulus
- Glaucoma
- Hereditary Glomerulopathy
- Hip Dysplasia
- Hypothyroidism
- Progressive Retinal Atrophy
- Pulmonary Stenosis

- Sebaceous Adenitis

In the following pages you will receive an overview of each of these conditions including their clinical signs and symptoms, methods for diagnosis, treatment options and prognosis information.

a.) Cataracts

Cataracts are characterized by an opacity in the lens of the eye which can obstruct the dog's vision. These opacities can be the result of disease, trauma, or old age and they can sometimes be inherited. For the most part, cataracts are not painful but they can sometimes luxate, or slip away from the tissue holding them in place and float around the eye. Sometimes they settle and block fluid drainage which can lead to glaucoma. Cataracts can't be prevented but vision loss can sometimes be corrected with surgery.

b.) Diabetes Mellitus

Also known as diabetes mellitus, diabetes is a condition that occurs when the dog's body fails to produce enough insulin or its sensitivity to insulin decreases. When your dog eats food, his body starts to break it down into glucose. In response to feeding, the body produces insulin which helps to carry the glucose into the cells where it can be used for energy. If the body doesn't produce enough insulin, or if it cannot use the insulin efficiently, blood glucose (or blood sugar) levels rise and cause a number of different complications.

There are two types of diabetes that dogs can get. Type 1 is inherited and it occurs when the dog's body cannot produce enough insulin. Type 2 is developed and it usually occurs when the dog's response to insulin becomes compromised – this is often correlated with obesity. Symptoms of diabetes in dogs may include changes in appetite, excessive thirst, weight loss, increased urination, lethargy, sweet-smelling breath, vomiting, and chronic skin infections.

Some dogs with diabetes must be given insulin injections to control their blood sugar levels. For others, weight loss and a healthy diet can reverse the effects of the disease. Type 1 diabetes cannot be prevented but a healthy lifestyle may help to prevent the development of Type 2.

c.) Gastric Dilation Volvulus

Also known as bloat, gastric dilation volvulus is a condition that most commonly affects large and giant breeds. Because the Samoyed is a fairly deep-chested breed, however, they are at risk as well. This condition occurs when the animals stomach fills with air and it twists on its axis, cutting off blood flow to and from the stomach. As the condition progresses, the abdomen fills with air and the organs and systems in the dog's body begin to break down from lack of oxygen and blood flow.

Some of the most common symptoms of gastric torsion in dogs include anxiety, depression, and abdominal pain or distended abdomen. Your dog may also start to drool excessively or vomit repeatedly. If the condition isn't corrected, his heart beat will become rapid and he will have trouble breathing. His pulse will weaken and he may fall into a coma or die suddenly.

The exact cause for this condition is unknown but certain things may increase the risk such as consuming large amounts of food or water in a short period of time. Strenuous exercise following a meal or swallowing too much air while eating can lead to gastric torsion as well. Immediate treatment is required to prevent death and surgical options are the most effective. Once treated, most dogs recover within a few weeks.

d.) Glaucoma

The Samoyed breed is prone to several eye-related conditions including glaucoma. Glaucoma is a very common condition in which the fluid inside the dog's eye builds and creates intraocular pressure that is too high. When the pressure inside the eye increases, it can lead to damage of the internal structures within the eye. If this condition is not treated promptly, it can lead to permanent loss of vision or total blindness for the dog.

There are two types of glaucoma – primary and secondary. Primary glaucoma involves physical or physiological traits that increase the dog's risk for glaucoma – this is usually determined by genetics. An example of a trait that might increase the dog's risk for glaucoma is small drainage pores that lead to accumulated fluid within the eye. Secondary glaucoma occurs when the glaucoma is caused by another condition such as a penetrating wound to the eye or other causes for inflammation.

Glaucoma can sometimes be difficult to diagnose in the early stages, but common signs include dilated pupil, cloudiness of the eye, and rubbing the eye. If you notice any of these symptoms, seek immediate treatment. Treatment options include topical solutions to reduce pressure, increase drainage, and to provide pain relief.

e.) Hereditary Glomerulopathy

Often nicknamed Samoyed hereditary glomerulopathy (or SHG) is an inherited renal disease that is also known as X-linked hereditary nephritis. The word "nephritis" refers to inflammation of the kidney and this disease generally causes progressive kidney dysfunction which often leads to kidney failure and death. This disease is X-linked in Samoyed dogs which means that male dogs are more likely to develop the disease and, if they do, it will generally be more severe than it is in females.

In many cases, the symptoms of Samoyed hereditary glomerulopathy develop very early. Common symptoms of SHG include excessive thirst and increased urination, vomiting, poor appetite, weight loss, lethargy, blood in the urine, and anemia. If allowed to progress, the disease will lead to a decrease in kidney function and eventual renal failure. In many cases, male Samoyeds affected by the disease die by the age of 15 months. The disease sometimes develops later and progresses more slowly in females.

Samoyed hereditary glomerulopathy is caused by a genetic defect carried on the X-chromosome – this is why it is sometimes called X-linked hereditary nephritis. This condition can be diagnosed through urinalysis, complete blood count, and other laboratory tests. Unfortunately, there is no cure for this disease but special diets may help to slow the progression and manage symptoms. Dogs that are carriers for the disease should not be bred.

f.) Hip Dysplasia

Hip dysplasia is a very common musculoskeletal problem among dogs. In a normal hip, the head of the femur (thigh bone) sits snugly within the groove of the hip joint and it rotates freely within the grove as the dog moves. Hip dysplasia occurs when the femoral head becomes separated from the hip joint – this is called subluxation. This could occur as a result of abnormal joint structure or laxity in the muscles and ligaments supporting the joint.

This condition can present in puppies as young as 5 months of age or in older dogs. The most common symptoms of hip dysplasia include pain or discomfort, limping, hopping, or unwillingness to move. As the condition progresses, the dog's pain will increase and he may develop osteoarthritis. The dog may begin to lose muscle tone and might even become completely lame in the affected joint.

Genetics are the largest risk factor for hip dysplasia, though nutrition and exercise are factors as well. Diagnosis for hip dysplasia is made through a combination of clinical signs, physical exam, and x-rays. Surgical treatments for hip dysplasia are very common and generally highly effective. Medical treatments may also be helpful to reduce osteoarthritis and to manage pain.

g.) Hypothyroidism

This condition is very common in dogs and it can produce a wide variety of symptoms. Hypothyroidism occurs when the thyroid gland fails to produce enough thyroid hormone – this often leads to weigh loss as well as hair and skin problems. Fortunately, this condition is easy to diagnose with a blood test that checks the dog's levels of certain thyroid hormones like T4.

The thyroid is a gland located in your dog's neck close to the voice box, or larynx. The activity of the thyroid is regulated by the pituitary gland in the brain which produces thyroid stimulating hormone (TSH). Hypothyroidism occurs when the thyroid produces insufficient thyroid hormone – this is most often caused by a destruction of the thyroid gland. This is often associated with other diseases like cancer or atrophy of the thyroid tissue. The use of certain medications can affect the thyroid gland as well.

Hypothyroidism is most commonly diagnosed in dogs between 4 and 10 years of age. The main symptoms of this disease include lethargy, hair loss, weight gain, excessive shedding, hyperpigmentation of skin, slow heartrate, high blood cholesterol and anemia. Treatment usually involves daily treatment with synthetic thyroid hormone.

h.) Progressive Retinal Atrophy

One of several eye problems seen in the Samoyed breed, progressive retinal atrophy (PRA) affects the retina of the eye - the part that receives light and converts it into electrical nerve signals that the brain interprets as vision. Dogs with PRA typically experience arrested retinal development (called retina dysplasia) or early degeneration of the photoreceptors in the eye. Dogs with retinal dysplasia usually develop symptoms within 2 months and are often blind by 1 year.

The signs of PRA vary according to the rate of progression. This disease is not painful and it doesn't affect the outward appearance of the eye. In most cases, dog owners notice a change in the dog's willingness to go down stairs, or to go down a dark hallway – PRA causes night blindness which can progress to total blindness. Unfortunately, there is no treatment or cure for progressive retinal atrophy and no way to slow the progression of the disease. Most dogs with PRA eventually become blind.

Fortunately, dogs often adapt well to blindness as long as their environment remains stable.

i.) Pulmonary Stenosis

Pulmonary stenosis is a congenital heart defect that is unfortunately fairly common in the Samoyed breed as well as the Cocker Spaniel, Boxer, Beagle, Chihuahua, and Mastiff. This disease is congenital (which means present at birth) and it is characterized by the narrowing of the pulmonary valve which results in decreased blood flow through the pulmonary artery into the right ventricle of the heart. This blockage can lead to anything from a minor murmur or arrhythmia to congestive heart failure.

There are three different types of pulmonary stenosis seen in dogs: valvular pulmonic stenosis, subvalvular pulmonic stenosis, and supravalvular pulmonic stenosis. The first of these is the most common. In mild cases of pulmonary stenosis, the dog may not show any symptoms but dogs that are severely affected may collapse suddenly or develop congestive heart failure. Some other symptoms may include abdominal distention, breathing difficulties, and exercise intolerance.

In addition to a thorough exam and history of symptoms, your veterinarian will perform a biochemistry profile to help diagnose pulmonary stenosis. The recommended course of treatment will vary depending on the severity of the condition but if the dog is suffering from congestive heart failure, hospitalization will be required. Balloon catheter dilation is sometimes used to fix an obstruction and advanced surgical techniques are sometimes used in more severe cases. The long-term treatment plan for this disease may involve medication and dogs with a mild form of the disease generally enjoy a normal lifespan.

j.) Sebaceous Adenitis

Sometimes known as inflammatory skin disease, sebaceous adenitis is a condition in which the sebaceous glands in the dog's skin become inflamed and die. In most cases, this disease is largely a cosmetic issue but it can cause extreme irritation. The most common symptoms for sebaceous adenitis in dogs include scaly skin, waxy or matted hair, dull coat condition, patches of hair loss, and inflammation. Symptoms of this disease usually appear on the head, neck, and back first, moving down the neck and along the back as it goes.

Unfortunately, there is no cure for sebaceous adenitis and secondary bacterial or yeast infections are common. It is also worth noting that this disease is fairly uncommon except in a few dog breeds including the Samoyed, Poodle,

Akita, and Old English Sheepdog. Treatment for sebaceous adenitis is usually focused on managing secondary infections. Frequent bathing with antimicrobial shampoo and use of topical medications may be helpful. Some dogs also respond well to fatty acid supplements.

Preventing Illness with Vaccinations

The best way to keep your Samoyed healthy is to provide him with a nutritious and balanced diet. You also need to ensure that he gets proper veterinary care, and that includes routine vaccinations. Vaccinations will not protect your Samoyed against nutritional deficiencies or inherited conditions, but they can help to protect him from certain communicable diseases like rabies, distemper, and parvovirus.

The vaccinations your Samoyed needs may vary depending where you live since certain regions have a higher risk for certain diseases. Your vet will know which vaccinations your dog needs and when he needs them, but the vaccination schedule below will help you to keep track of when your Samoyed needs to see the vet.

To give you an idea what kind of vaccinations your puppy will need, consult the vaccination schedule below:

Vaccination Schedule for Dogs**			
Vaccine	Doses	Age	Booster
Rabies	1	12 weeks	annual
Distemper	3	6-16 weeks	3 years
Parvovirus	3	6-16 weeks	3 years
Adenovirus	3	6-16 weeks	3 years
Parainfluenza	3	6 weeks, 12-14 weeks	3 years
Bordetella	1	6 weeks	annual
Lyme Disease	2	9, 13-14 weeks	annual
Leptospirosis	2	12 and 16 weeks	annual
Canine Influenza	2	6-8, 8-12 weeks	annual

** Keep in mind that vaccine requirements may vary from one region to another. Only your vet will be able to tell you which vaccines are most important for the region where you live.

Samoyed Care Sheet

By now it should be clear to you that the Samoyed is a beautiful and unique breed. Still, this breed does offer some challenges that need to be considered before you decide if it is the right breed for you. In making your decision you may wish to reference key pieces of information about the breed without flipping through the entire book to find them – that is where this Samoyed care sheet comes in. Here you will find all of the most relevant Samoyed facts and information separated into four sections for general info, habitat requirements, nutrition information and breed info.

1.) Basic Samoyed Information

Pedigree: Spitz-type breed developed by the Samoyedic peoples of Siberia for herding reindeer and pulling sleds

AKC Group: Working Group

Breed Size: medium

Height: 19 to 23.5 inches (48 to 60 cm)

Weight: 50 to 60 lbs. (23 to 27 kg)

Coat Length: medium-long; males have a ruff on the neck

Coat Texture: double coat; dense undercoat, long and coarse outer coat; stands away from the body

Shedding: heavy, frequent grooming needed; blows the coat once or twice a year

Color: solid white tipped with silver

Eyes and Nose: black or dark brown

Ears: small and pointed; prick ears

Tail: plumed and carried over the back

Temperament: sweet, affectionate, lively, playful, loyal, intelligent, trainable

Strangers: may bark at strangers but warms up quickly

Children: very good with children

Other Dogs: generally good with other dogs if properly trained and socialized

Training: intelligent and generally very trainable with time and consistency; positive reinforcement training is best

Exercise Needs: very active and energetic; 30-minute daily walk required with active playtime; may also appreciate training for work or dog sports

Health Conditions: hereditary glomerulopathy, diabetes, progressive retinal atrophy, pulmonary stenosis, hip dysplasia, sebaceous adenitis and hypothyroidism

Lifespan: average 12 to 14 years

2.) Habitat Requirements

Recommended Accessories: crate, dog bed, food/water dishes, toys, collar, leash, harness, grooming supplies

Collar and Harness: sized by weight

Grooming Supplies: wire pin brush, slicker brush, metal wide-tooth comb

Grooming Frequency: brush daily; professional grooming every 6 to 8 weeks

Energy Level: highly active

Exercise Requirements: 30-minute walk daily plus plenty of outdoor play time

Crate: highly recommended

Crate Size: just large enough for dog to lie down and turn around comfortably

Crate Extras: lined with blanket or plush pet bed

Food/Water: stainless steel or ceramic bowls, clean daily

Toys: start with an assortment, see what the dog likes; include some mentally stimulating toys

Exercise Ideas: play games to give your dog extra exercise during the day; train your dog for various dog sports

3.) Nutritional Needs

Nutritional Needs: water, protein, carbohydrate, fats, vitamins, minerals

Calorie Needs: varies by age, weight, and activity level

Amount to Feed (puppy): feed freely but consult recommendations on the package

Amount to Feed (adult): consult recommendations on the package; calculated by weight

Feeding Frequency: two to three meals daily

Important Ingredients: fresh animal protein (chicken, beef, lamb, turkey, eggs), digestible carbohydrates (rice, oats, barley), animal fats

Important Minerals: calcium, phosphorus, potassium, magnesium, iron, copper and manganese

Important Vitamins: Vitamin A, Vitamin A, Vitamin B-12, Vitamin D, Vitamin C

Look For: AAFCO statement of nutritional adequacy; protein at top of ingredients list; no artificial flavors, dyes, preservatives

4.) Breeding Information

Age of First Heat: around 6 months (or earlier)

Heat (Estrus) Cycle: 14 to 21 days

Frequency: twice a year, every 6 to 7 months

Breeding Age: at least 18 months to 2 years old, no more than 8 years old

Breeding Pair: both good examples of the breed standard; thorough DNA testing for hereditary conditions

Time Between Litters: at least one heat cycle, ideally one year

Greatest Fertility: 11 to 15 days into the cycle

Gestation Period: 61 to 65 days, average 63 days

Pregnancy Detection: possible after 21 days, best to wait 28 days before exam

Feeding Pregnant Dogs: maintain normal diet until week 5 or 6 then slightly increase rations

Signs of Labor: body temperature drops below normal 100° to 102°F (37.7° to 38.8°C), may be as low as 98°F (36.6°C); dog begins nesting in a dark, quiet place

Contractions: period of 10 minutes in waves of 3 to 5 followed by a period of rest

Whelping: puppies are born in 1/2 hour increments following 10 to 30 minutes of forceful straining

Puppies: born with eyes and ears closed; eyes open at 3 weeks, teeth develop at 10 weeks

Litter Size: 4 to 6 puppies, can be more or less

Size at Birth: about 12 to 17 ounces (340 to 480 grams)

Weaning: start offering puppy food soaked in water at 6 weeks; fully weaned by 8 weeks

Socialization: start as early as possible to prevent puppies from being nervous as an adult

Index

C

D

E

F

G

H

I

K

L

M

N

T

U

V

W

X

References

"AAFCO Dog Food Nutrient Profiles." DogFoodAdvisor.
<http://www.dogfoodadvisor.com/frequently-asked-
questions/aafco-nutrient-profiles/>

"Annual Dog Care Costs." PetFinder.
<https://www.petfinder.com/pet-adoption/dog-
adoption/annual-dog-care-costs/>

"Breed Origin and History." Samoyed Club of America.
<http://www.samoyedclubofamerica.org/the-samoyed/in-
depth/breed-origin-and-history/>

"Breed Standard." The Kennel Club.
<http://www.thekennelclub.org.uk/services/public/breed/st
andard.aspx?id=5139>

"Breeding Your Samoyed." Samoyed Club of America.
<http://www.samoyedclubofamerica.org/the-samoyed/in-
depth/breeding-your-samoyed/>

"Caloric Requirements for Your Dog." Tails.
<http://www.tails.co/requirements.html>

"Choosing a Healthy Puppy." WebMD.
<http://pets.webmd.com/dogs/guide/choosing-healthy-

"Congenital Heart Defect (Pulmonic Stenosis) in Dogs."
PetMD. <http://www.petmd.com/dog/conditions/
cardiovascular/c_dg_pulmonic_stenosis>

"Grooming Your Samoyed." Samsmiles.
<https://samsmiles.org/general-information/grooming-
your-samoyed/>

"Health Issues." Samoyed Club of America, Inc.
<http://www.samoyedclubofamerica.org/the-
samoyed/health-and-care/health-issues/>

"Hereditary Nephritis." Samoyed Club of America.
<http://www.samoyedhealthfoundation.org/diseases/hered
itary-nephritis>

"How to Find a Responsible Breeder." HumaneSociety.org.
<http://www.humanesociety.org/issues/puppy_mills/tips/f
inding_responsible_dog_breeder.html?referrer=https://ww
w.google.com/>

"My Bowl: What Goes into a Balanced Diet for Your Dog?"
PetMD. <http://www.petmd.com/dog/slideshows/
nutrition-center/my-bowl-what-goes-into-a-balanced-diet-
for-your-dog>

"Nutrients Your Dog Needs." ASPCA.org.
<https://www.aspca.org/pet-care/dog-care/nutrients-your-
dog-needs>

"Nutrition: General Feeding Guidelines for Dogs." VCA
Animal Hospitals. <http://www.vcahospitals.com/
main/pet-health-information/article/animal-
health/nutrition-general-feeding-guidelines-for-dogs/6491>

"Official Standard of the Samoyed." American Kennel Club. <http://images.akc.org/pdf/breeds/standards/Samoyed.pdf?_ga=1.140776754.1673202402.1466868664>

"Pet Care Costs." ASPCA.org. <https://www.aspca.org/adopt/pet-care-costs>

"Puppies." SamoyedMoms.com. <http://samoyedmoms.com/Puppies.html>

"Puppy Growth, Behavior, and Development." Sno Den Samoyeds. <http://snoden.org/puppy-growth-behavior-and-development>

"Puppy Proofing Your Home." PetEducation.com. <http://www.peteducation.com/article.cfm?c=2+2106&aid=3283>

"Puppy Weight Chart." Kenosha Samoyeds. <http://www.samoyed.org/Kenosha_Samoyeds/weight_chart.html>

"Samoyed." Dogtime.com. <http://dogtime.com/dog-breeds/samoyed>

"Samoyed." Vetstreet.com. <http://www.vetstreet.com/dogs/samoyed#overview>

"Samoyed Guide." Animal Planet. <http://www.animalplanet.com/breed-selector/dog-breeds/working/samoyed.html>

"Samoyed Temperament." Your Purebred Puppy. <http://www.yourpurebredpuppy.com/reviews/samoyeds.html>

"Sebaceous Adenitis in Dogs." Vetstreet.com. <http://www.vetstreet.com/care/sebaceous-adenitis-in-dogs>

"Vitamins and Minerals Your Dog Needs." Kim Boatman. The Dog Daily. <http://www.thedogdaily.com/dish/diet/dogs_vitamins/index.html#.VHOtMPnF_IA>

Feeding Baby
Cynthia Cherry
978-1941070000

Axolotl
Lolly Brown
978-0989658430

Dysautonomia, POTS
Syndrome
Frederick Earlstein
978-0989658485

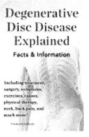

Degenerative Disc
Disease Explained
Frederick Earlstein
978-0989658485

Sinusitis, Hay Fever,
Allergic Rhinitis Explained
Frederick Earlstein
978-1941070024

Wicca
Riley Star
978-1941070130

Zombie Apocalypse
Rex Cutty
978-1941070154

Capybara
Lolly Brown
978-1941070062

Eels As Pets
Lolly Brown
978-1941070167

Scabies and Lice Explained
Frederick Earlstein
978-1941070017

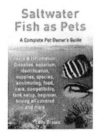

Saltwater Fish As Pets
Lolly Brown
978-0989658461

Torticollis Explained
Frederick Earlstein
978-1941070055

Kennel Cough
Lolly Brown
978-0989658409

Physiotherapist, Physical
Therapist
Christopher Wright
978-0989658492

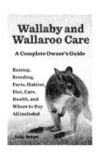

Rats, Mice, and Dormice
As Pets
Lolly Brown
978-1941070079

Wallaby and Wallaroo Care
Lolly Brown
978-1941070031

Bodybuilding Supplements
Explained
Jon Shelton
978-1941070239

Demonology
Riley Star
978-19401070314

Pigeon Racing
Lolly Brown
978-1941070307

Dwarf Hamster
Lolly Brown
978-1941070390

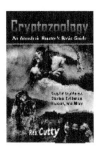

Cryptozoology
Rex Cutty
978-1941070406

Eye Strain
Frederick Earlstein
978-1941070369

Inez The Miniature Elephant
Asher Ray
978-1941070353

Vampire Apocalypse
Rex Cutty
978-1941070321

Printed in Great Britain
by Amazon

22742549R00079